HELLO, SUN- SHINE!

Just wanted you
to know I'm praying
for you today!

The Lord's love
His mercies never stop. They
LAMENTATIONS

JUST SO YOU KNOW:
It's going to be a good day!

Even if it doesn't feel like it,

God is

with You —

each and every minute of the

Day & Night.

I'm praying you feel Him with you
today and always.

He is always watching, never sleeping.
PSALM 121:3 TLB

JUST SO YOU KNOW:
There's never a single minute
when I'm not thankful for you
and loving you.

I prayed for you to

hEAR GOD'S VoiCE

today.

I pray
that the God who
gives hope will fill you with
much joy and peace while you trust
in Him. Then your hope will overflow by the
power of the Holy Spirit.

ROMANS 15:13 ICB

JUST SO YOU KNOW:
You ARE here today for a special purpose.

God knows you're not perfect.
He knows you make mistakes.

AND He
LΦVES
YOU

more than you can
possibly imagine.

I prayed for you to see yourself
the way He sees you today.

I am sure that God who began the good work
within you will keep right on helping you
grow in His grace.

PHILIPPIANS 1:6 TLB

JUST SO YOU KNOW:
I love watching how you are growing and growing!

I'm sorry you're struggling.
I'm praying God will show you how
BIG He is and how much

HE is on YOUR SIDE.

Give your worries to the Lord. He will take care of you.
PSALM 55:22 ICB

JUST SO YOU KNOW:
I'm proud of you, no matter what.

I'm praying for God to

give
you *the*
STReNGTH
You NEED

to do the work He's given you today.

Lord, You are my shield...
my wonderful God who gives me courage.

PSALM 3:3 ICB

JUST SO YOU KNOW:
I'm so proud of who you are and how you shine!

I prayed for God
to help you feel

BOUNCY
AND
HAPPY!
!!

and light on your
feet as you go
about your day.

God will yet fill your mouth with laughter.
And He will fill your lips with shouts of joy.

JOB 8:21 ICB

JUST SO YOU KNOW:
You make my heart smile.

YOU HAVE SO MANY TALENTS,

and I know the world will recognize them sooner or later.
I'm praying for sooner.

Just as there are many parts to our bodies, so it is with Christ's body. We are all parts of it, and it takes every one of us to make it complete.

ROMANS 12:4-5 TLB

 JUST SO YOU KNOW:
You're wonderful JUST
the way you are.

DaySpring

STEP
BY
STEP

and day by day, you're going to make it.
I asked God to give you patience until
you get there.

Better
to be patient than
powerful; better to have
self-control than to conquer a city.
PROVERBS 16:32 NLT

JUST SO YOU KNOW:
I believe in you!

Today, I asked God to remind you
how much you've accomplished.
You've come a long way—
but the best is yet to come!

Be HAPPY
AND FULL OF
JOY

because
the Lord has begun
to do wonderful things.

JOEL 2:21 ICB

JUST SO YOU KNOW:
God has big plans for you!

Life can be difficult,
choices can be hard,
and we all make mistakes.
But you can always remember that
God is full of

MeRcy
& L♥ve.

We can trust God.
I JOHN 1:9 ICB

I asked God to

TAKE

AWAY

all your worries and concerns today.

For God has not given us a spirit of fear
and timidity, but of power, love,
and self-discipline.

II TIMOTHY 1:7 NLT

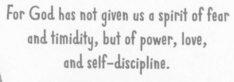

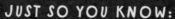

It might be hard to
see right now,
but you're on an

IMPORTANT
JOURNEY.

I'm praying God will
bring you joy,
peace, and understanding
along the way.

The Lord says, "I will guide you along the best pathway
for your life. I will advise you and watch over you."

PSALM 32:8 NLT

JUST SO YOU KNOW:
You are so strong and brave!

I asked God to help you keep count of the

GOOD
THINGS

He has given you.

Of course, there are way too many to count—
but it never hurts to try!

The joy of the Lord will make you strong.
NEHEMIAH 8:10 ICB

JUST SO YOU KNOW:
YOU are one of my very
favorite gifts.

I'm asking God to give you all kinds of

COURAGE,
HOPE, &
HAPPINESS

today.

With Him, nothing is impossible.
You've got this!

My God will
use His wonderful riches
in Christ Jesus to give you everything you need.

PHILIPPIANS 4:19 ICB

JUST SO YOU KNOW:
You're stronger than you realize
and more capable than you know.

I'm praying that you'll

STAY POSITIVE...

and that you'll never forget
I love you.

But if we look forward to something we don't yet
have, we must wait patiently and confidently.
ROMANS 8:25 NLT

JUST SO YOU KNOW:
Just by smiling, you can shift the mood of a room
or a conversation. Your smile changes the world.

I LOVE HOW YOU HELP OTHERS

with your God-given gifts and talents. I'm praising Him for you today.

Give, and you will receive. You will be given much. It will be poured into your hands—more than you can hold. You will be given so much that it will spill into your lap. The way you give to others is the way God will give to you.

LUKE 6:38 ICB

JUST SO YOU KNOW:

You have a special purpose in this world, and the best part is, you don't have to figure it out. Jesus will show you.

I prayed for you to feel God's hug today.

HE IS HOLDING YOU

with His strong, loving arms.
Do you feel it?

Come near to God,
and God will come near to you.

JAMES 4:8 ICB

JUST SO YOU KNOW:
God's hugs are real, and mine are too.
Come get one anytime.

I know you're
feeling overwhelmed,
and that's normal
sometimes.
Today I'm praying

YOU FEEL
REFRESHED

like a big glass of cool
water on a
hot day.

The Lord is my shepherd.
I have everything I need.
PSALM 23:1 ICB

JUST SO YOU KNOW:
God never feels overwhelmed,
and He can lead you through this with joy.

I can tell

YOU'RE
REALLY
TRYING.

I pray (and I believe) that your
hard work will be rewarded. Soon!

Be strong and courageous, and do the work. Don't
be afraid or discouraged, for the LORD God, my
God, is with you. He will not fail you or forsake you.
I CHRONICLES 28:20 NLT

JUST SO YOU KNOW:
How you treat others today
matters more than
your test scores.

I asked God to GUIDE YOUR STEPS today.

The Lord
will always lead you.
He will satisfy your needs in dry
lands. He will give strength to your bones.
You will be like a garden that has much water.
You will be like a spring that never runs dry.

ISAIAH 58:11 ICB

JUST SO YOU KNOW:
You carry the love of Jesus today,
and you're going to get to share it with others.

I prayed for God to give you

EVERY-THING YOU NEED

for today.

Do not worry about anything.
But pray and ask God for everything you need.

PHILIPPIANS 4:6 ICB

JUST SO YOU KNOW:
You don't ever need to feel like you're not good enough.
You've got access to God's toolbox, and that is full of everything you need
to share His love and get through today with joy and strength!

I asked God to

Open Your HearT

to accept His forgiveness.
Mistakes happen, but He never
wants us to be ashamed.
He has forgiven you,
so it's time to forgive yourself.

We pray that the LORD will lead your hearts into God's love
and Christ's patience.

II THESSALONIANS 3:5 ICB

JUST SO YOU KNOW:
You're loved more than you think you are.

I prayed for God to remind you that He not only knows your future but...

HE PLANNED IT.

"For I know the plans I have for you," says the LORD. "They are plans for good and not for disaster, to give you a future and a hope."

JEREMIAH 29:11 NLT

JUST SO YOU KNOW:
God made you on purpose. You're one-of-a-kind on purpose.
Your life has incredible value, because He says so.

DaySpring

You know what you
need to do, but it's not
going to be easy.
I'm asking God to give you the

CONFI-
DENCE
& COURAGE

to take that first step.

Be strong and brave. Don't be afraid...don't be frightened.
The Lord your God will go with you.
He will not leave you or forget you.

DEUTERONOMY 31:6 ICB

JUST SO YOU KNOW:
God has already equipped you for
what you will face today.

I asked God to give you the power to

FACE
ALL YOUR
FEARS

and to overcome them once and for all.

I will not be afraid because the Lord is with me.
People can't do anything to me.

PSALM 118:6 ICB

JUST SO YOU KNOW:
Sometimes fear is a chance for
you to experience the joy of trying
something hard and doing it well.

DaySpring

Today, I prayed for God to open your eyes to the

BEAUTY OF HIS CREATION.

Be on the lookout for a rainbow, a colorful tree, or a blooming flower— He put it there for you to enjoy.

Let the skies rejoice and the earth be glad. Let the sea and everything in it shout. Let the fields and everything in them show their joy. Then all the trees of the forest will sing for joy.

PSALM 96:11-12 ICB

JUST SO YOU KNOW:
God cares more about you than you could possibly imagine.

Today I told God how

THANKFUL
I AM FOR
YOU!

And I want you
to know it too.

You have a special place in my heart.
PHILIPPIANS 1:7 NLT

JUST SO YOU KNOW:
You have an impact on the people around you,
much more than you know.

Think HAPPY THOUGHTS today.

I'm praying—and I truly believe—
that the better days will be here sooner
than you think.

The mountains may disappear, and the hills may come to an end.
But My love will never disappear.

ISAIAH 54:10 ICB

JUST SO YOU KNOW:
What you're going through is temporary.
God WILL make a way.

L♥VE
neVeR
ENDS.

So I'm praying that you'll remember
we love you. Always.

No one has ever seen God.
But if we love each other, God lives in us,
and His love is brought to full expression in us.

I JOHN 4:12 NLT

JUST SO YOU KNOW:
If they lined up a million kids and let me choose,
I'd always choose you.

I asked God
to remind you that no challenges
are too big for Him.

EVEN
BIG
PROBLEMS
ARE NO
PROBLEM
FOR GOD.

I can do all things through Christ because
He gives me strength.

PHILIPPIANS 4:13 ICB

JUST SO YOU KNOW:
The joy of the Lord is going to
help you through today.

CONGRAT-ULATIONS!

Your hard work has paid off.
I'm praying that you'll enjoy
every minute of what God has done
through you.

Those who plan and work hard earn a profit.
PROVERBS 21:5 ICB

JUST SO YOU KNOW:
I'm so proud of you for working
hard and doing your best.

DaySpring

The Lord knows that when
He made you, He created a

One
of a
KIND

treasure.
I pray that you'll know how
special you are too.

You
made my whole
being. You formed me in my
mother's body. I praise you because
you made me in an amazing and wonderful way.
What you have done is wonderful.

PSALM 139:13-14 ICB

JUST SO YOU KNOW:
You know what? I really like you.

God has
BIG
PLANS
FOR YOU

and very important work that only you can do.
I'm praying that you and God will
make the most of your talents.

God had special plans for me even before I was born.

GALATIANS 1:15 ICB

Today, I asked God to give you

STRENGTH
& COURAGE.

Lots of both.
And know what?
I think He's already
answering my prayer.

I asked the Lord for help, and He answered me.
He saved me from all that I feared.

PSALM 34:4 ICB

JUST SO YOU KNOW:
God's opinion of you matters more than
anyone else's, even your friends'.

DaySpring

Every day, including this one,
is a chance to begin something new.
I'm praying for your

FRESH
START.

This is the day that the Lord has made.
Let us rejoice and be glad today!

PSALM 118:24 ICB

JUST SO YOU KNOW:
You're growing up so well—
I know you're going to make it in life!

I asked God to

GIVE YOU WIS-DOM

for the decisions ahead.
I knew that you could make
good choices, but I figure that
you and God together can
make great ones.

God began doing a good work in you.
And He will continue it until it is finished...I am sure of that.

PHILIPPIANS 1:6 ICB

JUST SO YOU KNOW:
Jesus will help you focus on
others' needs more than your own.

WE'RE THANKFUL FOR YOU

and we pray for you every single day.

Children are a gift from the Lord.

PSALM 127:3 ICB

JUST SO YOU KNOW:
You're not alone, wherever you go
and whatever you do. God goes with you.
He watches over you and guides you. You have
the ability to hear Him and follow His lead.

DaySpring

I pray that you'll keep

THINKING GOOD THOUGHTS.

It doesn't cost anything to be positive, and it's a lot more fun than "stinkin' thinkin'!"

So you will
go out with joy.
You will be led out in peace.
ISAIAH 55:12 ICB

JUST SO YOU KNOW:
Someone today is facing a very dark moment.
Jesus is placing you there for it.

Today, I prayed for you to

STAY 💪

STRONG.

There's nothing you'll face today that
you and God, working together,
can't handle.

Depend on the Lord and His strength. Always go to Him
for help. Remember the wonderful things He has done.
Remember His miracles and His decisions.

PSALM 105:4-5 ICB

JUST SO YOU KNOW:
God is using today's challenges to grow you
into the best possible person!

You're getting closer to the

FINiSH

LINe!

I asked God to help you
finish strong and soon.

We must not become tired of doing good.
GALATIANS 6:9 ICB

JUST SO YOU KNOW:
If you weren't my kid,
I'd want one as great as you.

You've been getting ready for

THIS

ADVENTURE,

and now you've begun.
Congratulations!
I'm praying for you.

The Lord will always lead you.
ISAIAH 58:11 ICB

JUST SO YOU KNOW:
God is using you to be a light for Him.

Nothing is too hard for God,
and miracles happen every day.

Big
MIRACLES.

LittLe
MiRacLeS.

In-between ones too.
I'm praying for yours.

No one has ever seen this. No one has ever heard about it.
No one has ever imagined what God has
prepared for those who love Him.

I CORINTHIANS 2:9 ICB

JUST SO YOU KNOW:
I'm hugging you in my heart today.

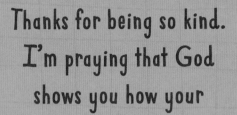

Thanks for being so kind.
I'm praying that God
shows you how your

KiNDNESS
MaTTERS.

I love you....You bring me joy and
make me proud of you.
PHILIPPIANS 4:1 ICB

 JUST SO YOU KNOW:
You're making a difference,
more than you know.

Prayer is a WORRY-Extinguisher.

Whenever you're worried
(or whenever you're not!),
it's a good time to pray.

Do
not worry
about anything. But
pray and ask God for everything
you need. And when you pray, always give
thanks. And God's peace will keep your hearts and
minds in Christ Jesus. The peace that God gives is so great that
we cannot understand it.
PHILIPPIANS 4:6-7 ICB

JUST SO YOU KNOW:
Jesus is always there and always listening to your prayers.
Even when you can't hear Him, He can hear you.

I prayed that you'll feel God's peace in

BIG WAYS today.

I leave you peace. My peace I give you. I do not give it to you as the world does. So don't let your hearts be troubled. Don't be afraid.

JOHN 14:27 ICB

WIDER

THAN THE

WIDEST RIVER.

Deeper than the deepest ocean.
Able to reach from Jesus in heaven,
straight to you, with a single prayer.
That's the power of His love.
And I pray it fills you up today.

We pray that the Lord will lead your hearts into
God's love and Christ's patience.

II THESSALONIANS 3:5 ICB

JUST SO YOU KNOW:
You *matter* to Jesus.

"I'LL BE PRAYING FOR YOU!"

More than just a nice thing to say—I really mean it.

I always thank my God
when I pray for you.
PHILEMON 1:4 NLT

JUST SO YOU KNOW:
Whenever you're ready to talk, I'm ready to listen.
I'm here for you no matter what.

I know the perfect Person to call—and

His Line is NEVER BUSY.

Pray to Me, and I will answer you. I will tell you important secrets. You have never heard these things before.

JEREMIAH 33:3 ICB

JUST SO YOU KNOW:
Jesus is always with you, always hears you when you pray, and always cares about what you have to say.

You've got some things to think about,
and I know it's not easy.
I asked God to guide you and

SHOW you
THE WAY.

Trust the Lord with all your heart.
Don't depend on your own understanding.
Remember the Lord in everything you do.
And He will give you success.

PROVERBS 3:5-6 ICB

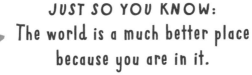

JUST SO YOU KNOW:
The world is a much better place
because you are in it.

I'm praying for you to see
God's plan for you, to know it,
and to follow it with

ALL

YOUR

HeART.

I am
the light of the
world. The person who
follows Me will never live in darkness.
He will have the light that gives life.

JOHN 8:12 ICB

JUST SO YOU KNOW:
You're such an encouragement to me and others
as you live life trusting God.

GOD
IS
WORKING

in ways you can't see—
in ways you can't even imagine!

God began doing a good work in you. And He will
continue it until it is finished when Jesus Christ
comes again. I am sure of that.

PHILIPPIANS 1:6 ICB

JUST SO YOU KNOW:
You're doing GREAT. For real.

Whatever comes your way today,
I'm praying that you'll sense
God's still, small voice saying,

"YOU are MINE. I L♥VE YOU."

Nothing now, nothing in the future, no powers, nothing above us, nothing below us, or anything else in the whole world will ever be able to separate us from the love of God that is in Christ Jesus our Lord.

ROMANS 8:38-39 ICB

JUST SO YOU KNOW:
Just be you. You don't need to try to be anyone else.

God will always do what's

BEST
FOR US.

Even if the path feels unsettled,
when we step forward He turns
our feet in the right direction.
Today I prayed that the way
to go would be obvious for you.

I will be glad because of Your love....
You have set me in a safe place.

PSALM 31:7-8 ICB

JUST SO YOU KNOW:
I'll help you through this as you go.

I'm lifting you up in prayer...because

you're SPECIAL

and because I care.

Two people are better than one.
They get more done by working together.
ECCLESIASTES 4:9 ICB

JUST SO YOU KNOW:
Every day is a chance to begin something new,
to try again, and to hope for big things.

I know at times it can be very hard to do the right thing,
especially when it seems like everyone around you
is doing what you know is wrong.
I asked God to help you want to do things well and

MAKE
GOOD
CHOICES.

We should make plans—
counting on God to direct us.

PROVERBS 16:9 TLB

JUST SO YOU KNOW:
You are a bright spot in
so many people's days.

I wish hurts never happened and I could

MAKE
EVERYTHING
BETTER
WITH A
HUG.

I asked God to hold you close today.

Lord,
I know that
Your laws are right....
Comfort me with Your love,
as You promised me.

PSALM 119:75-76 ICB

JUST SO YOU KNOW:
I wish other parents could have
a kid as great as you.

When I'm praying for you,
I ask God to give you a little
something that lets you know there's
nothing He'd rather do

THAN TAKE CARE OF YOU.

I pray that from His glorious, unlimited resources He will
empower you with inner strength through His Spirit.

EPHESIANS 3:16 NLT

JUST SO YOU KNOW:
God has chosen you and set you apart for His purposes.

I prayed today that the
God of grace would show you what

A BLESSING
YOU
are.

He is the faithful God.
He will keep His agreement of love for a thousand lifetimes.
DEUTERONOMY 7:9 ICB

JUST SO YOU KNOW:
Your friends are blessed to have you.

JUST WHAT YOU NEED.

just when you need it.
That's what I'm praying for you.

Not a single sparrow can fall
to the ground without your
Father knowing it.

MATTHEW 10:29 NLT

JUST SO YOU KNOW:
If you see someone hurting in need, God may have put you there
just so you can help them. And He'll help you do it.

You're going to make it through this because of who you are and Whose you are.

It's a

PROMISE FROM GOD

and a prayer by me!

But in all these things we have full victory through God who showed His love for us.

ROMANS 8:37 ICB

JUST SO YOU KNOW:
You're making more of a difference than you realize.

I asked God
to share  **His**

joy

with you today—
joy that doesn't make sense—
silly joy that makes your day the best.

May the Lord bless and protect you; may the Lord's
face radiate with joy because of you.

NUMBERS 6:24 TLB

JUST SO YOU KNOW:
I like you just the way you are.
God will continue growing you, but
meanwhile, don't change yourself!

PRAYING the LORD CHEERS You UP TODAY

and lets you see yourself as He sees you.

The Lord
gives strength to His
people. The Lord blesses His
people with peace.

PSALM 29:11 ICB

JUST SO YOU KNOW:
You let Jesus shine when you look people
in the eyes and smile.

Good Things are Ahead

just you wait and see.

I've asked God today to help you see, very soon.

The God who comforts them will lead them.
He will lead them by springs of water.

ISAIAH 49:10 ICB

YOU MAKE THIS WORLD A BETTER PLACE

just by being you.
I told God, "Thanks,"
because you make my life better too.

Sing to the Lord a new song because He has done miracles.
By His right hand and holy arm He has won the victory.

PSALM 98:1 ICB

JUST SO YOU KNOW:
It's okay to step away from situations you don't like.
Sometimes silence speaks louder than words.

L♥Ve
J☀Y
PEACE
PATIENCE
KINDNESS

I've asked God to give you a little helping of whatever you need today.

My God will use His wonderful riches in Christ Jesus to give you everything you need.

PHILIPPIANS 4:19 ICB

JUST SO YOU KNOW:
You have unlimited resources from God, and all you have to do is ask Him.

DaySpring

I asked God to make you
excited about your

DREAMS
& HOPES

today.
He is painting an amazing
future for you.

We know that in everything God works for
the good of those who love Him.

ROMANS 8:28 ICB

JUST SO YOU KNOW:
If I were your age,
I'd want to be your best friend.

I'M BELIEVING WITH YOU

in all the great things God can do!

I am the Lord. I am the God of every person on the earth.
You know that nothing is impossible for Me.

JEREMIAH 32:27 ICB

 JUST SO YOU KNOW:
I like the way you handle yourself.
You are growing in wisdom!

CONSIDER THIS A
HUG

that you can take with you.
And a promise that I'm praying
for you all day long.

I pray
that God, the source
of hope, will fill you completely
with joy and peace because you
trust in Him.

ROMANS 15:13 NLT

JUST SO YOU KNOW:
You are doing great.
You're not screwing anything up. Really!

Things are changing quickly for you right now. Today I asked God to

SURROUND YOU WITH HIS peace

that passes all understanding.

And God's peace will keep your hearts and minds in Christ Jesus. The peace that God gives is so great that we cannot understand it.

PHILIPPIANS 4:7 ICB

JUST SO YOU KNOW:
It's okay to just be still for a while and take a break.

the
LORD
iS
FAITHFUL

to meet our needs—
and everything is sure to come out just right.
I asked God to help you hang in
there until you see it!

My grace is enough for you. When you are weak,
then My power is made perfect in you.

II CORINTHIANS 12:9 ICB

JUST SO YOU KNOW:
I not only love you, but I really like you too.

I may not understand exactly what you're going through, but I know that

GOD
goes THROUGH
EVERYthing
WITH YOU.

And I've asked Him to stick close with you today.

He will not leave you or forget you.
DEUTERONOMY 31:6 ICB

JUST SO YOU KNOW:
An honest answer to a tough situation always shows God's grace.

The moments of your
day and the

NEEDS OF
YOUR
HEART

are in God's hands—
and in my prayers.

Give all your worries to Him, because He cares for you.
I PETER 5:7 ICB

JUST SO YOU KNOW:
Be the kind of friend you're looking for,
and you'll find the very best friends.

Today I prayed for you, because

GOD
KNOWS
JUST WHAT
TO DO.

Give your worries to the Lord. He will take care of you.
He will never let good people down.

PSALM 55:22 ICB

 JUST SO YOU KNOW:
You never, ever need to
worry or be afraid.

You've got a

SPECIAL
PLACE

in God's heart...
and in my prayers.

I thank
God every time I
remember you. And I always
pray for all of you with joy.
PHILIPPIANS 1:3-4 ICB

JUST SO YOU KNOW:
There is always, always someone thinking
about you and loving you!

I asked God to remind you
all day today how much

HE ♥'s

you.

Nothing can separate us
from the love God has for us.

ROMANS 8:38 ICB

I prayed that God would

hold YOUR HAND

throughout your day today!

The Lord says, "I called you to do right. And I will hold your hand.
I will protect you....You will be a light to shine for all people."
ISAIAH 42:6 ICB

JUST SO YOU KNOW:
Everyone else around you wants to be loved and accepted too.
You can go first and make their day.

Hope is being excited for the good and even miraculous things God will do. I asked God to

FiLL YOU WiTH HiS HOPE TODAY!

There is a right time for everything. Everything on earth has its special season.

ECCLESIASTES 3:1 ICB

JUST SO YOU KNOW:
Smiling and laughing are great ways to lift your mood, even when you don't feel like it.

Today I thanked God
(as I do every day!) for

WONDER-
FUL,
AMAZING
YOU.

God looked at everything He had made, and it was very good.

GENESIS 1:31 ICB

JUST SO YOU KNOW:
You have gifts that only you
can give the world.

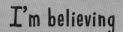

I'm believing

GREAT THINGS FOR YOU!

I am certain that God, who began the good work within you,
will continue His work until it is finally finished.

PHILIPPIANS 1:6 NLT

JUST SO YOU KNOW:
I care about everything that
matters to you. I'm here to help!

When your heart is hurting (ouch!)
and your head is spinning (whew!)
and your world seems upside down
(what happened?)
I'm here for you (anytime!)

& the

LORD
iS TOO
(aLWaYs!).

The Lord
your God is with
you. The mighty One will save
you. The Lord will be happy with you.
ZEPHANIAH 3:17 ICB

JUST SO YOU KNOW:
God is only a prayer away.

I asked God to help you

KNOW

the

TRUTH

about things and to be flexible and
open to others' viewpoints.

Light shines on those who do right.
Joy belongs to those who are honest.

PSALM 97:11 ICB

JUST SO YOU KNOW:
You don't have to be cool, popular, or trendy.
You'll attract the best friends if you're just genuine and kind.

Today I asked God to put
someone in your path who

needs
your
CHEER.

You are the light that gives light to the world.
MATTHEW 5:14 ICB

JUST SO YOU KNOW:
Look people in the eyes. Smile. Say nice things.
Your day—and life—will be WAY richer for it.

Understanding what others mean is
more important than being understood.
I'm asking God to help you

 GROW

iN WISDOM &

UNDERSTANDING.

You are young, but do not let anyone
treat you as if you were not important.
Be an example.

I TIMOTHY 4:12 ICB

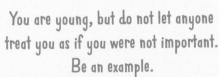

JUST SO YOU KNOW:
It's okay to ask questions. Lots of questions.

I'm praying that you

HAVE FUN.

Not just work.
Even if you're not at recess.
God can make life fun!

Ask and you will receive. And your joy will be the fullest joy.
JOHN 16:24 ICB

JUST SO YOU KNOW:
Learning to laugh at yourself and
situations is a valuable gift!

DaySpring

I'm asking God to heal you
completely and quickly—

HE CAN
DO IT!

But for you who honor Me, goodness will shine on you like
the sun. There will be healing in its rays.

MALACHI 4:2 ICB

JUST SO YOU KNOW:
You'll be stronger when you're well
than before you got hurt.

Losing can be so hard
when you care so much.
I'm asking God to give you

His
PEACE &
UNDERSTanding.

The
Lord is close
to the brokenhearted.
PSALM 34:18

JUST SO YOU KNOW:
It might be hard to believe right now, but good
things will come of this if you stay close to God.

I don't know what I'd do without your
help—and I'm making sure God knows

HOW
THANKFUL
I AM!

I thank God for the help you gave me.
PHILIPPIANS 1:5 ICB

JUST SO YOU KNOW:
When you're kind, the whole
world gets a little brighter.

Feeling jealous is normal.
I've asked God to help you

CELEBRATE

the

GOOD NEWS

of others and enjoy the good things in
your own life as well.

Be happy with those who are happy.
ROMANS 12:15 ICB

JUST SO YOU KNOW:
There are times when you get what others
around you want, and they struggle with jealousy too.

Today I asked God to give you
just what you need to succeed.

I BELIEVE
iN YOU,

and I know He does too!

God has given each of you some special abilities.
I PETER 4:10 TLB

JUST SO YOU KNOW:
Just do your best—and you might just be
surprised at what you can accomplish.

You are BRAVE. You ARE STRONG.

And I'm asking God to remind you of this, right when you need it most.

But for God all things are possible.

MATTHEW 19:26 ICB

JUST SO YOU KNOW:
Sometimes bravery means doing the things you don't want to do—hard things—but God is with you especially in those times.

I'm setting my alarm to go off every hour,
to remind me to pray for you

ALL
day Long.

I will pray morning, noon, and night...
and He will hear and answer.
PSALM 55:17 TLB

JUST SO YOU KNOW:
You were made for just this
day and moment.

Worrying is a waste of time...
but it's so hard not to do.
I'm asking God to help you

Focus on the GOOD

and give your worries to Him.

Continue
to think about the
things that are good and
worthy of praise. Think about the things
that are true and honorable and right and pure
and beautiful and respected.

PHILIPPIANS 4:8 ICB

JUST SO YOU KNOW:
God thinks about you all the time and
wants to see you happy.

HELLO, SUN-SHINE!

I've asked God to keep your day bright
and full of good things!

Every good action and every perfect gift is from God.
These good gifts come down from the
Creator of the sun, moon, and stars.

JAMES 1:17 ICB

JUST SO YOU KNOW:
You matter more than you think you do!

God will always help you

Do WHAT'S RighT.

I've asked Him to
show you the way.

I will strengthen you; I will help you;
I will uphold you with My victorious right hand.
ISAIAH 41:10 TLB

JUST SO YOU KNOW:
It's always easier to follow the crowd.
But you'll like yourself better if you follow Jesus.

Lord, the person holding
this paper is

one
OF MY
FAVORITES.

Please pour out your good gifts today!

Every good action and every
perfect gift is from God.

JAMES 1:17 ICB

JUST SO YOU KNOW:
Trying to fit in is overrated, because you
already fit perfectly. Just be yourself.

I asked God to help you

FEEL HIS LOVe TODAY

and help you notice the people around you who need to feel loved too.

Cheerful givers are the ones God prizes.
II CORINTHIANS 9:7 TLB

JUST SO YOU KNOW:
Sharing and being generous makes others—and YOU—feel amazing.

I asked God to bring

HAPPY, FUNNY, SILLY

thoughts to your mind.

Be full of joy in the Lord.
PHILIPPIANS 3:1 ICB

 JUST SO YOU KNOW:
When you smile or laugh,
it lights up a whole room.

Do you know

HOW

L♥VEd

you

are?

I asked God to help
you understand.

God loves
you. And we know
that He has chosen you
to be His.

I THESSALONIANS 1:4 ICB

JUST SO YOU KNOW:
You bring me so much joy!

God really outdid Himself when He made
you—and we're so happy you were born
into this family! Thank You, Lord, for this

AMAZING
KID.

You made my whole being.
You formed me in my mother's body.
PSALM 139:13 ICB

JUST SO YOU KNOW:
We are celebrating you today!

DaySpring